YOUR KNOWLEDGE HAS VALUE

- We will publish your bachelor's and master's thesis, essays and papers

- Your own eBook and book - sold worldwide in all relevant shops

- Earn money with each sale

Upload your text at www.GRIN.com
and publish for free

Matin Wasiri

A Comparison of Robert Frost's "The Hill Wife" and "Stopping by Woods on a Snowy Evening" with Regard to the Representation of Nature

GRIN Verlag

Bibliografische Information der Deutschen Nationalbibliothek:

Die Deutsche Bibliothek verzeichnet diese Publikation in der Deutschen National-
bibliografie; detaillierte bibliografische Daten sind im Internet über http://dnb.d-
nb.de/ abrufbar.

Imprint:

Copyright © 2012 GRIN Verlag GmbH
Druck und Bindung: Books on Demand GmbH, Norderstedt Germany
ISBN: 978-3-656-47024-3

This book at GRIN:

http://www.grin.com/en/e-book/230552/a-comparison-of-robert-frost-s-the-hill-
wife-and-stopping-by-woods-on

GRIN - Your knowledge has value

Der GRIN Verlag publiziert seit 1998 wissenschaftliche Arbeiten von Studenten, Hochschullehrern und anderen Akademikern als eBook und gedrucktes Buch. Die Verlagswebsite www.grin.com ist die ideale Plattform zur Veröffentlichung von Hausarbeiten, Abschlussarbeiten, wissenschaftlichen Aufsätzen, Dissertationen und Fachbüchern.

Visit us on the internet:

http://www.grin.com/

http://www.facebook.com/grincom

http://www.twitter.com/grin_com

Matin Wasiri   28/02/2012

A Comparison of Robert Frost's "The Hill Wife" and "Stopping by
Woods on a Snowy Evening" with Regard to the Representation
of Nature

When comparing Robert Frost's poems "The Hill Wife" and "Stopping by Woods on a Snowy Evening", the first thing that strikes the eye is what ominous and dark connotations the simplest natural events seem to carry. In his poem "The Hill Wife", Robert Frost invokes a theme of peril by giving a sense of foreboding to everyday occurrences in a married couple's life. These occurrences are mostly physical and biological events, such as the swarming of birds, the dark in the night, or the scratching on windows of branches moved by the wind. One occurrence however – though not unambiguously so – hints at the reason of the later death of the woman. This incident involves a supposed pedlar, whose smile's sincerity the woman does not trust when she states "that smile! It never came of being gay" (24). She even suspects him of "watching from the woods" (34) and of having "a vision of us old and dead" (32). When in the end, the woman first is lost and later buried, her husband "learned of finalities / Besides the grave" (73-4). In "Stopping by Woods on a Snowy Evening", the plot is far more simple, as it basically only illustrates the melancholic rumination on seclusion, civilisation, the temptation of release, and the purpose of continuing life with all its duties of a person standing in the woods. This is done in a rather emotional way, since the logical reflections are not explained, but rather the general mood is illustrated poetically.

In the beginning of "The Hill Wife", Robert Frost describes the birds going and coming, the respective emotional interpretation of their behaviour by the inhabitants of the house, as well as their criticism with how important they deem this animal behaviour:

One ought not to have to care

1

So much as you and I

Care when the birds come round the house

To seem to say good-bye;

Or care so much when they come back

With whatever it is they sing;

The truth being we are as much

Too glad for the one thing

As we are too sad for the other here--

With birds that fill their breasts

But with each other and themselves

And their built or driven nests. (1-12)

The criticism here lies in the last three lines, where the musing leads to
the conclusion that all worries and joys connected to the birds'
behaviour are a waste, if one considers that these beasts are only
concerned "with each other and themselves" (11). Furthermore,
however gloomy nature is portrayed in most of the poem's parts, the
fourth stanza contrasts two different kinds of darkness, and the fact that
they were "preferring the out- to the in-door night" (20) reveals that
within the house threats are presumed by the couple. This positive
relativisation of nature's dangerousness is reversed in the next stanza,
in which the dubious vagrant is supposed to be "watching from the
woods" (34). However, nature here is not hazardous on its own, but
rather through a human being possibly lingering within it. The
personified branches brushing against the windows are then even

2

compared to another element of nature, a little bird, in these lines:

> The tireless but ineffectual hands
>
> That with every futile pass
>
> Made the great tree seem as a little bird
>
> Before the mystery of glass! (39-42)

Quite obviously this reflects the anxiety of the inhabitants of unknown danger surrounding their house, who probably are not actually "afraid [...] / Of what the tree might do" (45-6), but are rather generally nervous of lurking danger, possibly in shape of the derelict. Finally, in the last part "The Impulse", the man loses his wife, first to the woods, not knowing about her whereabouts, but later he becomes certain about her death and the manner in which she was killed ("he learned of finalities / Besides the grave", 73-4). Later "she ran and hid / In the fern" (65-6), which symbolises nature as a protective factor.

In "Stopping by Woods on a Snowy Evening", Robert Frost expresses a feeling of solitude by letting the first-person narrator depict his struggle with succumbing to the charms of the forest – the leaving behind of earthly matters – when he states that he is about to "watch his woods fill up with snow" (4), indicative of a rather lengthy time window. The fact that these woods belong to a person the narrator knows, and that "he will not see me stopping here" (3) represents a direct connection between the nature depicted and the civilised world, which can potentially be left behind. Only his horse keeps him from doing that, when "he gives his harness bells a shake / To ask if there is some mistake" (9-10), while "the only other sound's the sweep / Of easy wind and downy flake" (11-2), noises close to tranquillity. As a working

3

animal, the horse is unmistakably an element which builds the bridge between nature and mankind, "think[ing] it queer / To stop without a farmhouse near" (5-6). On the other hand, the calm woods seem to represent death, being "lovely, dark and deep" (13), but also potentially hindering him from getting the "miles to go before I sleep" (15) behind him.

When comparing the two poems directly, three aspects can be found that are prominent in both of them with regard to Frost's utilisation of nature-based metaphors – darkness, the woods, and personified constituents of nature. These three elements all are described with varying nuances of connotation, which clearly add to the poems' respective overall atmospheres. For "The Hill Wife" that is an atmosphere of uneasiness, an air of temptation to rest forever for "Stopping by Woods on a Snowy Evening".

When Frost describes the woods' darkness in "Stopping by Woods on a Snowy Evening" by saying that they "are lovely, dark and deep" (13), he makes it seem highly appealing for the traveller tired of the cold. Although this darkness carries a promise of demise in the form of death, the lonesome wanderer seems to regret his obligations, when his musing about the loveliness of the dark woods is opposed to the fact that he has "promises to keep" (14). In a similar way, darkness is connoted in "The Hill Wife" by contraposing "the out- to the in-door night" (20). Just as in the other poem, the darkness to be found in nature is depicted with a positive undertone when it says that the couple "learned to leave the house-door wider / Until they had lit the lamp inside" (21-2).

4

The woods as an entity are related to death in both poems. But the reception of death is expressed with different implications. In "Stopping by Woods on a Snowy Evening", Robert Frost relates the deep woods to a peaceful death, as is expressed by the repeated mantra within which death is identified as sleep ("and miles to go before I sleep, / And miles to go before I sleep" 15-6). In "The Hill Wife", on the other hand, the woods – though maybe tranquil in nature, too – are populated by at least one violent human counterpart, transforming the incomplete solitude within the woods into a dangerous status. The fact that the suspicious vagrant is "watching from the wood as like as not" ("Hill Wife" 34) as well as the wife's final passing both suggest a violent death. Thus, peaceful and violent deaths are discerned by Robert Frost with regard to the darkness of woods. While the first is harmless and even appealing, the other carries dire consequences.

The traveller's companion in "Stopping by Woods on a Snowy Evening" is a horse whose demeanour and movements are read as communication attempts when the protagonist speculates on its thoughts ("my little horse must think it queer / To stop without a farmhouse near" 5-6), and whose movements are interpreted as reservation towards the stopping in the wilderness when "he gives his harness bells a shake / To ask if there is some mistake" (9-10). The horse acts as a connecting link between nature and human civilisation, it is aware of the perils within nature and warns against them. In "The Hill Wife", the personification of the branches trying to invade the couple's house is different to the horse in that the tree is a natural entity that is not used to man's ways, but is rather "as a little bird / Before the

5

mystery of glass" (41-2).

The proprietisation of nature through mankind is portrayed in both poems, and although nature carries risks as well, in both poems the human influence is considered as something negative. In "Stopping by Woods on a Snowy Evening", the human world is considered the disturbing element, while nature promises calm and relaxation, albeit a permanent one. In "The Hill Wife", however, nature is by and large a source of strong uneasiness, but the real danger is a human being that uses nature's cover to do evil. Thus, although expressed in different ways, Robert Frost describes nature in both poems as something positive, with human influence obstructing or completely obliterating its innate merits.

CITED WORKS

Frost, Robert. "Stopping by Woods on a Snowy Evening." *Collected Poems*. Cutchogue, NY: Buccaneer Books, 1986. 275. Print.

Frost, Robert. "The Hill Wife." *Collected Poems*. Cutchogue, NY: Buccaneer Books, 1986. 160-62. Print.